THE ART OF HOOKED-RUG MAKING

THE *ART* OF HOOKED-RUG MAKING

BY MARTHA BATCHELDER

Cover photographs by Peter E. Randall

Copyright © 1947 by Martha Batchelder
Reprinted 1983
ISBN 0-89272-138-3
Library of Congress Catalog Card Number 83-70934

5

Down East Books, Camden, Maine

I dedicate this book to the
memory of my brother, Paul.

M.R.B.

Contents

Suggestions
From the Designer's Notebook

Do you have the urge to do creative work? You have creative ability, though you probably do not know it and will be surprised when your unsuspected talents come to light. They are there just waiting to be uncovered.

WHY DESIGN YOUR OWN RUGS?

I often think of a Bible verse, Jeremiah 33:3: "Call unto me, and I will answer thee, and show thee great and mighty things, which thou knowest not." That means *you* — the talents are at your disposal if you will only claim them and use them!

Many people are content to let someone else do their thinking for them, not realizing that what they do themselves gives them more pleasure and satisfaction.

We live in a world where things are standardized. So, when you make a rug, do not try to copy a commercial rug; make something different, something you have always liked and wanted.

When you see "custom made" on an article, you expect it to be different from and superior to the machine-made article and to cost more. Your rugs are *custom made*. Keep that fact always in mind.

My water-color teacher told me I had it in me if I could only get it out. I say the same thing to you — get it out!

Whenever you see a small sketch, design, or picture that you like, cut it out and save it. It may be a border, an arrangement of flowers or a single flower, a corner, a silhouette — anything that appeals to you.

When you have a lot saved, put them into large envelopes. Mark on the outside *Borders, Scrolls, Corners, Flowers,* etc., or paste the very small pieces on cards or slip them into books. I have several books full of cuttings, besides the envelopes.

Be on the lookout all the time for material; the magazines and papers are full of suggestions. Greeting cards will give you lots of ideas. You can get ideas from dishes or wallpaper.

MATERIAL FOR RUG BACKING

Burlap comes in three widths — 36, 40, and 48 inch. Use the very best quality that you can get; you are putting many hours of work into any rug that you make and the best is none too good.

Grain bags are strong and make good foundations for simple designs but are hard to draw on when it comes to difficult designs. The average grain bag is 40 inches wide and about 50 inches long. Beet pulp also comes in very large bags, 40 inches wide and 84 inches long, and if you can get a good one it will work very nicely. Diamond walnuts come in very nice, large bags.

Look your material over very carefully before you rip a bag apart. Many of them are mended or otherwise imperfect. Use only the good ones.

Many people wash burlap bags to get the dirt out. I never have, thinking it would take out the sizing. During the war, the bags were so coarse that I did it to tighten the mesh. Now you can get good burlap bags.

1. Cut all burlap along a thread.

2. Turn under ¼ to ½ inch and stitch on machine.

3. Put your burlap on a table or floor, and with a yardstick find the middle lengthwise. Mark a line, with a sharp-pointed pencil, at this point between threads the whole length of the burlap. Get the middle crosswise the same way.

In all your measuring, work from these two lines.

4. *Putting Design on Burlap.* Put your burlap on a table. If you are going to do a geometric, put your pattern over one space, slip the carbon paper under and hold or pin it in place, and go over all the lines with a blunt-pointed pencil, bearing down hard. Do the same all over, remembering to reverse the pattern where called for in the design.

When doing other kinds of designs, put the full-size pattern over the burlap, with the middle and crosswise lines of the pattern on the same lines of the burlap. You can put flatirons or something else heavy on one part to hold it in place while you slip the carbon underneath the spot where you are tracing, or you can pin the carbon and pattern sheets together at tracing spots.

5. Ink all lines, using a coarse lettering pen and any ink. Do not have sunshine on work while you do this.

6. *Putting Rug in Frame.* Find the middle of the listing on one side of your frame and make a mark. Pin the center of the short side of your burlap to this. Thread a coarse needle with string and, starting from this point, begin sewing toward the end. Do the same to the other half; then sew other side of burlap in.

Decide what part of your rug you are going to work on first. If a geometric, start at one end, but work from the center first with other designs.

Roll your rug around the frame and fasten the frame together. See Figure 1.

Run shoe lacings through the sides of rug and tie to the sides of frame.

7. When you have the part hooked that shows in the frame, untie the shoe lacings, take out the pins, roll up what you have done, and work on another part.

8. When your rug is finished, rip from listing, trim burlap all around — leaving one inch of burlap — turn under, and press with a not-too-hot iron.

Take a piece of rug binding (it comes in various colors and is $1\frac{1}{4}$ inches wide) long enough to go around your rug. Face your rug with this binding and give it a good pressing with a not-too-hot iron. You must face your rug. If you do not, it will go to pieces when the burlap edges that are turned under get worn.

For further instructions, in detail, see Lesson 3, "A Border Design," and Lesson 4, "Geometrics."

RUG FRAMES

There are a number of good frames on the market. Use the one you like best. Many people use strips of wood held together by clamps. See Figure 2. I like the one in the sketch. It is made of two pieces of wood $1\frac{3}{4}$ inches square. A slot is cut in each end large enough for strips of wood $\frac{3}{4}$ inch by $1\frac{3}{4}$ inches to go through. You can see in the sketch how the pieces go together. Holes are bored in the strips that go through the end slots, and pins hold them in place.

The sketch shows where the listing should be tacked.

You can have this frame in different sizes. For 40-inch burlap, have the end pieces 48 inches long and the sides set at $41\frac{1}{2}$ inches from slot to slot.

You can use the same frame for 36-inch material, but the strips might as well be 4 inches shorter so the frame will not take up so much room. I have one 35 inches long for small rugs. Of course, any length frames can be made. You can use the same side pieces for all of them.

You can draw your burlap as tight as a drum on this frame without someone to help you.

Side

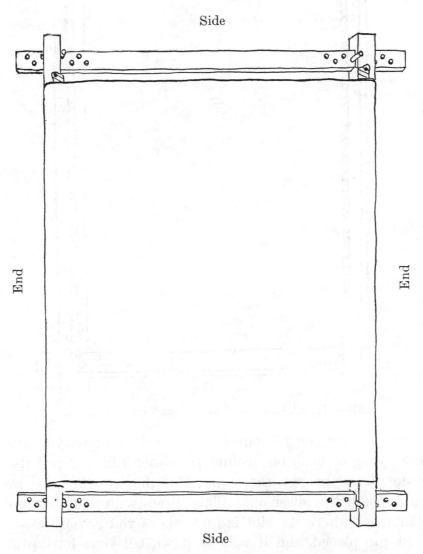

End

End

Side

FIGURE 1. You can get your burlap as tight as a drum. Put three pins in; then stand frame up and press with foot on lower corner where you have no pin. Press till burlap is taut; then put the last pin in.

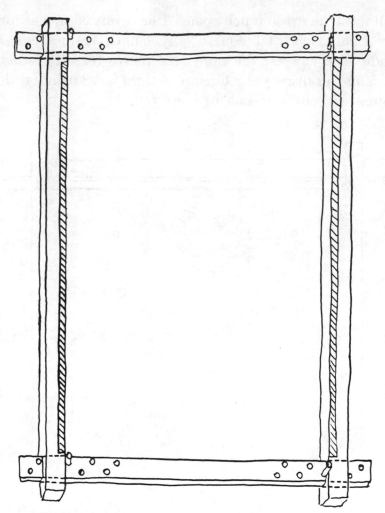

FIGURE 2. How the frame looks with last pin in.

Sew your rug to your listing. Roll the part you are not going to hook on around the other end and put the side pieces through the slots. Put the two top pins in and one of the lower ones. Then press with your foot on the piece where the slot is and where you haven't your last pin placed, and it will go down till your burlap is taut and you can slip the last pin in. See Figure 1.

Tie the edges of the burlap to the sides of the frame with shoe lacings.

I lean my frame against a very high sawhorse, but you cannot carry that around with you. One ingenious lady devised legs to fasten to the side pieces — two strips 1¾ inches square and 27 inches long, with a round pin glued in a hole in the end of each. These pins slip through the holes in the side pieces of your frame.

One of the best features of this frame is that you can unroll your rug and spread it out on the floor whenever you want to.

HOOKS

There are a number of different kinds of hooks. I use my grandmother's. She had them made by the local blacksmith. Some people have crochet hooks set in a handle. Use the hook that you like best. See Fig. 5.

Lesson 1
Hooking Your First Rug

Mᴀᴋᴇ your first rug a small one and use a simple design. The main idea at first is to learn to hook well. You do not want to have to think about a pattern, but to be free to concentrate on even hooking. You can finish a small rug quickly, and not get discouraged as you might if you tried a large one first.

A good rug for you to begin on is the one shown in Figure 3, with a border around the edge and small spaces in the center. The one shown is 24½ inches wide and 36 inches long. To make it, get 29 inches of 40-inch-wide burlap and do steps 1, 2, and 3.

MEASURING

Measure from lengthwise center 12¼ inches both ways, and from crosswise center 18 inches. Make pencil line around these points.

Measure in 4 inches all around for border. Then, from outside going in, measure 1⅛ inches, ⅝ inch, ¾ inch, ⅝ inch, and ⅞ inch. Mark with pencil lines. The threads of the burlap vary, so you cannot be too exact about this.

With black crayon, divide the center up into irregular shapes. Make it like one of the crazy quilts they used to make. Put in a triangle, then a lopsided square and a five-sided affair, and so on. If some of the spaces are too big, break them up with a line. Do steps 5 and 6.

FIGURE 3. This interesting, mosaic-like pattern makes a rug with no top or bottom. Looks all right from any direction.

HOOKING

Look through your scrap wool pieces. *Use nothing but wool in a rug.* For the border, you will need a lot of black, some tweed or plaid mixture, and a light color. You can use these also in the center, but there you will need some bright and dull colors.

You must have a theme color — just as you hear a recurrent theme in a symphony, so you have a color that you keep repeating at intervals throughout your rug.

Cut your material about ¼ inch in width, depending on the weight. Tear your material so as to get a straight edge to cut from when cutting long strips as you do for your border.

Sit in a low, comfortable chair with no arms. Sit way

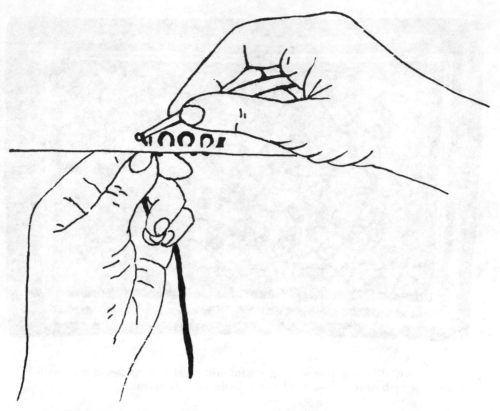

FIGURE 4. The hooking process, from a cut-through sideview.

back in the chair. Put a chair or low stool at your right to hold your scissors, which you must never keep in your lap.

You are now ready to start hooking.

Hooking the Border

Start on the inside of the border, as the lines are straight here and you can follow a thread.

Take a strip of black material between the first and second fingers of your left hand and hold it under the right-hand side of the inside line of the border.

Grasp the hook in your right hand and push it through between the threads at the place where your left

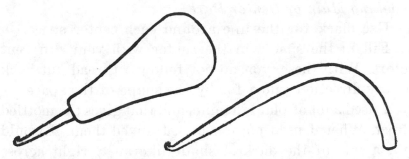

FIGURE 5. Two good hooks. Author uses the curved type.

hand holds the material. See Figure 4. Then pick up a piece of the material with the hook and pull it through so that you make a loop about ⅓ to ½ inch above the burlap. *(Some do not pull it up so high. You will have a tendency at first to pull it higher than after you have been hooking awhile.)* Skip two threads and, following the line going from right to left, put the hook down and pull up another loop. Keep on pulling the loops up to the same height on top till you have the line all hooked and are ready for a new line.

Look on the wrong side to be sure that there are no loops there and that it is smooth.

Since all pieces are joined on the right side, the ending of each piece must come there, too. It will be slow work at first, but keep on practicing and soon you can do it quickly.

Skip two threads and do the second row and then the third. Four rows should fill the first border space inside. If they do not, put in another row.

Now put a row of light color next, then a row of tweed or plaid mixture and another row of the light, to fill the second border space.

Fill in the next space with black; three rows should be enough. Then put in your tweed or plaid mixture and, finally, use black in the outer space or edge. Five rows should fill this.

Hooking Main or Center Part

Use black for the line around each center space.

Fill in the spaces in the center with your different colors. With these, you do not follow a thread but hook in any direction called for by the shape of the space.

I used a lot of plaid in mine, and that gives the mottled effect. When I used plain colors, I mixed them. I would run a line of the darkest shade like an S right across the center part of the space and then run the other shades of the same color around it to fill. If the space was large enough, I would put a touch of that dark shade in again. I love to run shades of blue and green in together. When filling in, remember to "break joints," as my mother calls it. Run one color for a little way, then start another; *but do not start it where the other leaves off.* Start back a little and then run in where the other stops. Try it yourself and you will see.

Remember to keep repeating your theme color, to mix your bright and dull colors and your dark and light, and not to have too much of any one color in any part of your rug.

And above all use the colors you like! If you don't do it now, you will never be happy till you do!

Judging Your Work

Stand your rug up against the wall while working and look at it from a distance every once in a while, to be sure that you have your bright and dull colors well mixed.

Trimming the Ends at the Joints

Train yourself not to put your hook down and pick up your scissors to trim off every end. Let them alone and do a lot at one time.

Do step 8.

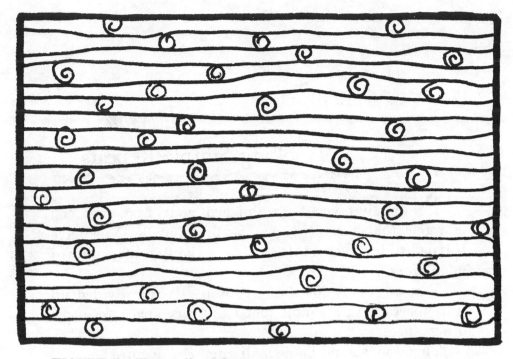

FIGURE 6. The curlicue design — much more attractive in a finished rug with right colors than here.

Alternative "First Pattern"

Another nice rug to do at first is one with uneven lines and curlicues going from one to the other. See Figure 6. Make your lines and curves black. Plaids, checks, or mixed colors would be nice for the rest.

Lesson 2
Hooking Simple Repeats

Now that you have finished your first rug, you can feel that you are over the first hurdle. You have learned to hook smoothly, which is the first step toward good work.

You are ready for the next step — a rug divided up into spaces with a simple motif in every space, or every other space.

This, too, should be a small rug. See Figure 7.

PLANNING RUG SHOWN IN FIGURE 7

This is 5 units wide and 7 long, as it is more pleasing to the eye to have an uneven number.

Take 28 inches of yard-wide burlap and do steps 1, 2, and 3.

Starting from the lengthwise center, measure either way about 2½ inches, then about 5 inches. From the other center, do the same.

DESIGNING

Fold a piece of paper about 5 inches square twice and cut patterns till you have one that you like.

Do steps 4, 5, and 6.

HOOKING

I outlined each unit in black and made the center

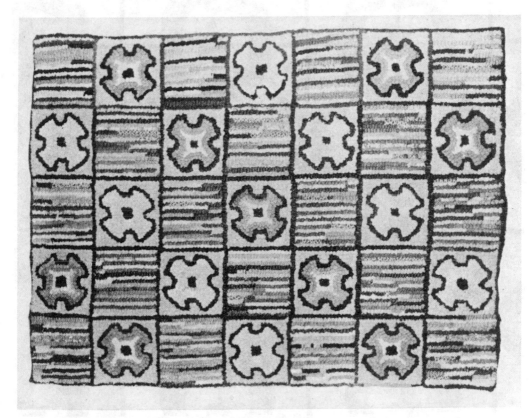

FIGURE 7. Pattern in a simple motif, repeated in every other space. Colors can vary as shown.

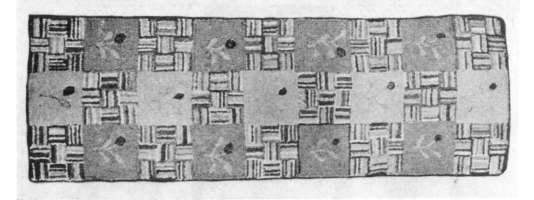

FIGURE 8. Simple pattern, with bud and leaf worked in. HOOKED BY MRS. DAVID F. BATCHELDER.

[23]

FIGURE 9. Basic pattern for a simple geometric.

FIGURE 10. For discussion of hooking lettering, see the lessons on Welcome mats and wall hangings.

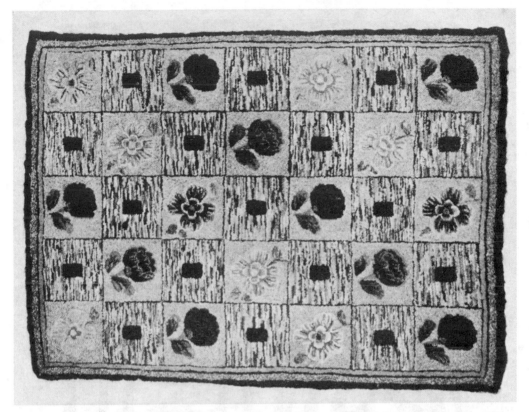

FIGURE 11. The effect of working still more detail into the simple motif shown in Figure 7. HOOKED BY MRS. FORREST CHASE.

black, then went around that with cream and went out a little at each corner for the points. Then I filled in between with dark blue in one, light blue in the other.

In the alternate squares, I used hit-or-miss colors — just mixed colors I had, using some of the blues. I used tan for background.

Do steps 7 and 8.

Figure 8 shows a rug which my mother made for a certain place in a hall.

PLANNING RUG SHOWN IN FIGURE 8

Take a piece of 36-inch burlap 57 inches long and cut a strip off the side so that your strip is 21 inches wide.

FIGURE 12. This has been hooked and sold. Another example of the alternate-square motif.

Do steps 1, 2, and 3.

Starting from lengthwise center, measure 3 inches either way, then 6 inches. Starting from crosswise center, measure the same.

It is 18 inches wide and 54 inches long.

DESIGNING

Cut paper the same size as the squares. In one put

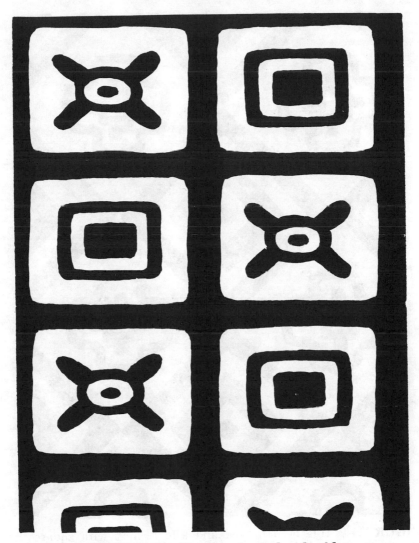

FIGURE 13. Has been hooked and sold.

a stem, leaves, and bud, and divide the other up into nine spaces.

Do steps 5 and 6.

HOOKING

The buds in this rug are red, the leaves and stems bright green; the background of one type is light tan

FIGURE 14. Has been hooked and sold. Effect with squares arranged to show as diamonds.

and the other brown. The colors used in the hit-or-miss,
which is hooked different ways to make one part look
as though it lapped over the other, are partly bright, to
make stripes, and the other colors are mixed in.

The rug has faded and the colors are much softer
than when it was first hooked.

Do steps 7 and 8.

FIGURE 15. Another variation of squares, with corners clipped.
HOOKED BY MRS. DAVID F. BATCHELDER.

Figure 9 shows a design that would be easy to do.

Figure 10 shows how your initial could be used in a square. You could have a dark color and then a light for the background. And use any combination for the initials. One could be dark and one light, or a plaid could be used.

A rug made from a 7-inch square with flowers in one and hit-or-miss in the other is shown in Figure 11.

Figures 12, 13, and 14 show designs which I have hooked and sold.

Figure 15 shows a rug based on squares. Pieces of paper were folded and the corners cut off. Then stars were cut and put in part, and the rest had simple designs in them.

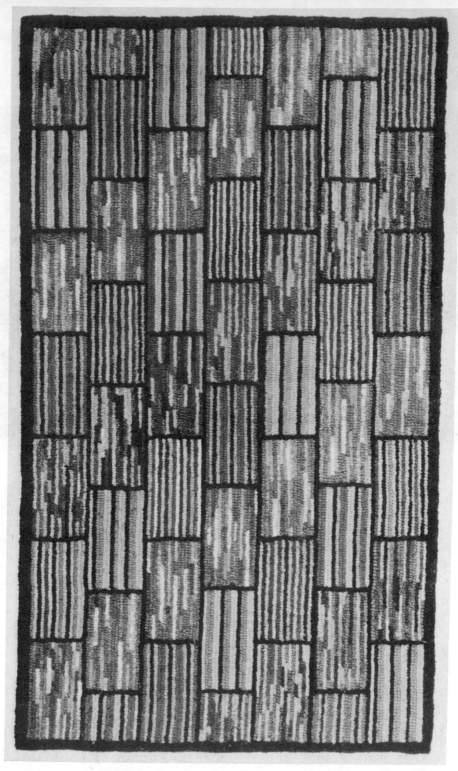

FIGURE 16. One of three of the author's rugs shown in McCall
Needlework.—PRINTED BY COURTESY OF THE MC CALL CORPORATION.

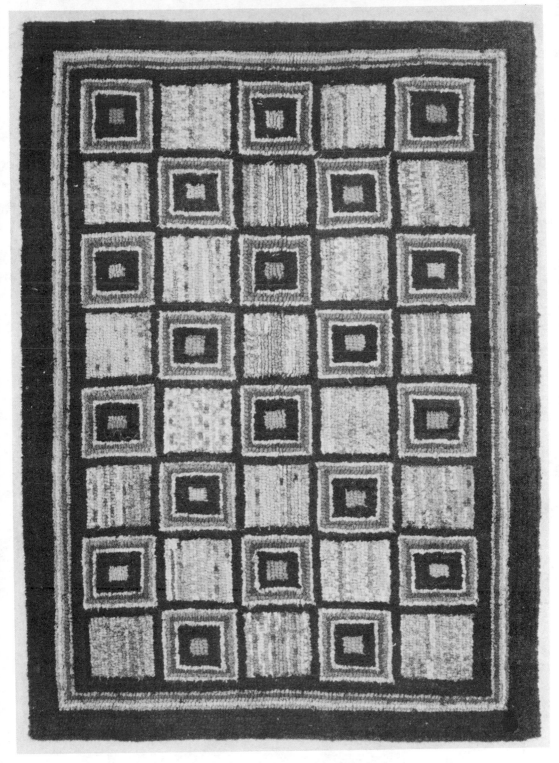

FIGURE 17. Another of the author's rugs from McCall Needlework.
—PRINTED BY COURTESY OF THE MC CALL CORPORATION.

A brick rug will give you a chance to use up a lot of your pieces of bright colors. Every other brick is a mixed tan or gray. See Figure 16.

Figure 17 — a rug you will like to make. The dark was a very old dark green serge. In the center of the squares, bright red and green were used.

Lesson 3

Hooking a Simple Border

⟨decorative rule⟩

THE rug shown is just a little harder to hook than the one shown in Lesson 1. See Figure 18.

It is 23 inches wide and 35 inches long. To make this, get 26 inches of yard-wide burlap and do steps 1, 2, and 3.

MEASURING

(Figure 19A, B, C, D, E, and F)

Measure $11\frac{1}{4}$ inches each way from the center for the width and $17\frac{1}{4}$ inches each way for the length. This will give you the outside measurements of your rug. Figure 19A.

Starting from the two center lines and working out, measure $2\frac{1}{2}$ inches and $8\frac{3}{4}$ inches each way, Figure 19B; next get $3\frac{5}{8}$ inches and $9\frac{5}{8}$ inches, Figure 19C; then $4\frac{3}{4}$ inches and $10\frac{3}{4}$ inches, Figure 19D.

Measure out $5\frac{1}{2}$ inches both ways from the last line shown in Figure 19D and divide this space in half with a line, Figure 19E.

Figure 19F shows all lines as they will look on your material. Ink all pencil lines.

DESIGN FOR BORDER

(Figure 20A, B, C, D, E, and F)

You are now ready to make the design for your border, which will fit in the space shown in Figure 19E.

FIGURE 18. A handsome rug, somewhat more advanced than the square-motif type. The drawings in Figure 19 show how this rug was measured and the design laid out, except for the border, which is covered in Figure 20.

Take a piece of thin brown paper and measure as shown in Figure 20A, and cut on the outside line. This will fit into one fourth of the space on your rug; try it on the rug to be sure that it fits all right. Crease from A to B and from B to C. Divide space from C to D into three equal parts and do the same from A to E. Draw a pencil line through creases. Figure 20B.

Draw in one half of your corner design and then fold on crease. Put piece of carbon underneath and trace off the other half. Top, Figure 20D. At the top of Figure 20C, you will see three spaces. Your pattern must fit into two of these, and half must go in the other one. Trace two on a small piece of paper to practice on.

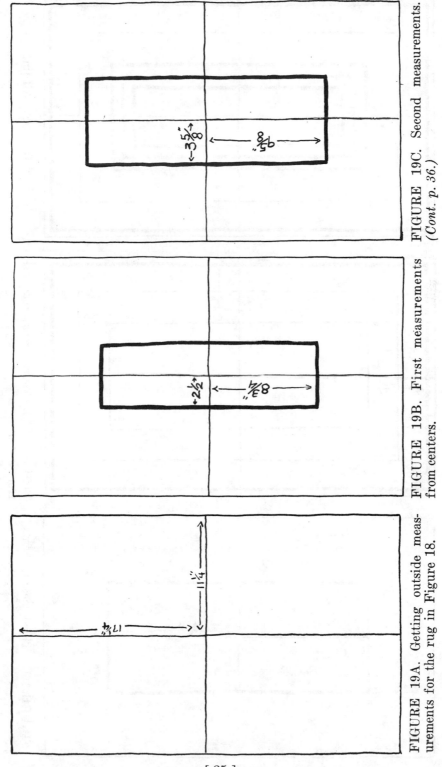

FIGURE 19A. Getting outside measurements for the rug in Figure 18.

FIGURE 19B. First measurements from centers.

FIGURE 19C. Second measurements. *(Cont. p. 36.)*

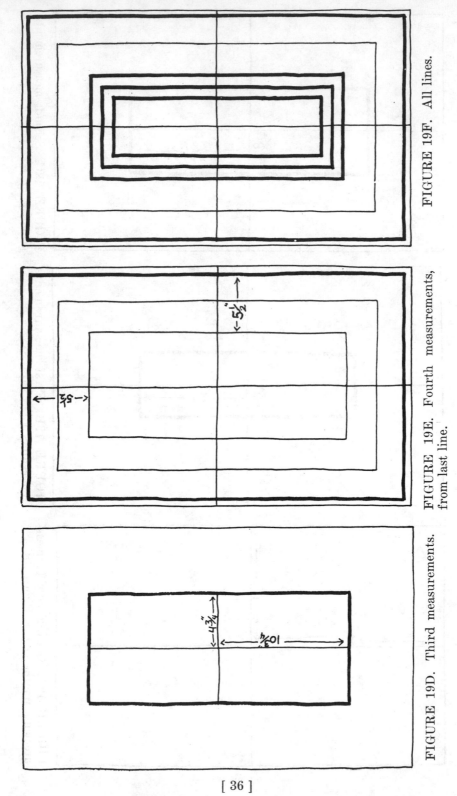

FIGURE 19F.   All lines.

FIGURE 19E.   Fourth measurements, from last line.

FIGURE 19D.   Third measurements.

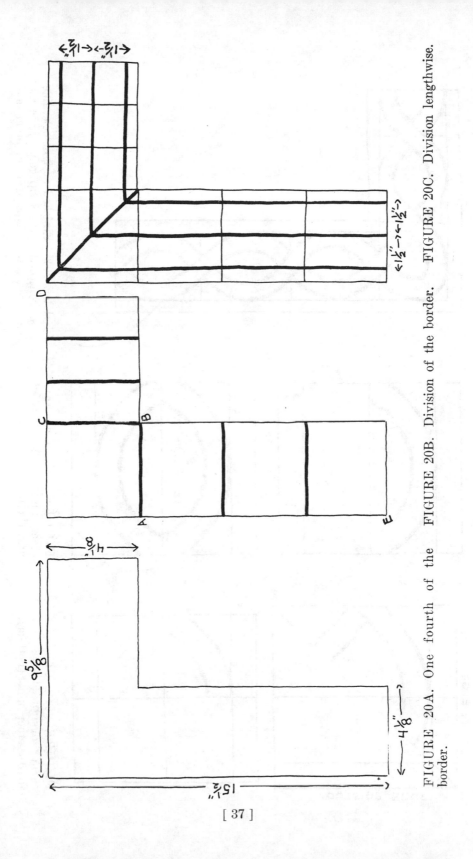

FIGURE 20A. One fourth of the   FIGURE 20B. Division of the border.   FIGURE 20C. Division lengthwise.
border.

[37]

FIGURE 20F. Finished design looks like this. Notice that the strip going from the center out always laps over the other one.

FIGURE 20E. One half other unit (top); finished unit (bottom).

FIGURE 20D. One half corner design (top); one fourth other unit (bottom).

OUTSIDE EDGE

OUTSIDE EDGE

Fold on lines and draw in one corner first, Figure 20D; then trace onto the other half, transfer this half, and you have the whole design, Figure 20E.

Try your pattern in the spaces. One half should fill the half space. The top spaces are just a bit wider than the ones at the sides, and you will have to take a tiny tuck in the center to make it fit in these spaces.

Do steps 4, 5, and 6.

MAKING THE RUG

Look through your woolen pieces and decide what colors you want to use.

In the finished rug, Figure 18, the border shown in Figure 20F was done in shades of green, and there was a band of the same between the first two lines from the center. The four heavy lines in Figure 19F were done in white. Inside the pointed ovals in the border was a row of white, one of henna, one of light blue, and the center was black. Black was used between the second and third lines from the center (with a row of henna next to the inside) and on the outside of the rug.

Outside the ovals in the border was a row of white — one of brown, one of yellow, and the rest a brown mixture.

In the center inside the white line was a row of brown, one of yellow, and the rest of brown mixture.

Do step 7 and, when finished, step 8.

Lesson 4
Designing With Geometrics

T̲o̲ ᴍᴀᴋᴇ a good-sized geometric based on a square, take 58 inches of 36-inch burlap and do steps 1, 2, and 3. From the center both ways, measure 5½ inches, then 11 inches, till you have three spaces one way and five the other each 11 inches square. The outside measurements will be 33 x 55 inches.

DESIGNING

You are now ready to make your design. From thin brown paper, cut a number of 11-inch squares.

In Figure 21 are shown steps in making a simple design in a square.

1. Take an 11-inch square, crease in middle both ways and then crosswise.

2. Open it out and it will look like A, Figure 21.

3. Fold again and draw in the design shown in B.

4. Open out, place carbon underneath, and trace to the other half of square, as in C.

5. Put carbon underneath and trace to the other half, as in D.

6. Do the same and you will get E.

7. Take a 22-inch square, divide into four parts, draw lines, and transfer E on to the four squares.

F shows how four of the units look together.

Where the four corners meet, you will need something. Make a diamond to fit in the space.

FIGURE 21. Designing a geometric based on a square. For a similar design on a finished rug, see Figure 22.

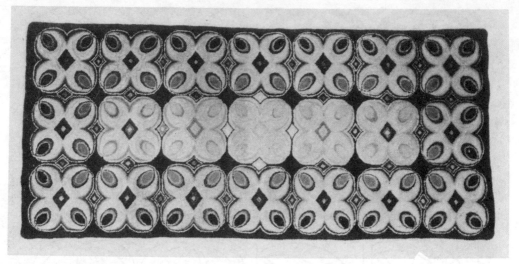

FIGURE 22. Geometric based on a square. Size, 34½ by 77 inches.
HOOKED BY MRS. ARTHUR PRICE.

G shows how the design would look with the curved part dark.

H — with the background dark and the curved part a lighter shade.

Figure 22 shows a rug made from a similar design. The outside units are all the same color, but the five in the center are shaded from the ends toward the center.

The lady who made it said that before she put in the frame she marked the center unit "1," the two next "2," and the last "3." In this way she could tell when to start shading.

In Figures 23, 24, 25, 26, and 27, you will see designs based on this same 11-inch square.

A rug hooked from the design worked out in Figure 28 is shown in the photograph, Figure 30. Note richness of finished effect.

Choose the design that you like best and transfer to thin brown paper.

Do steps 4, 5, and 6.

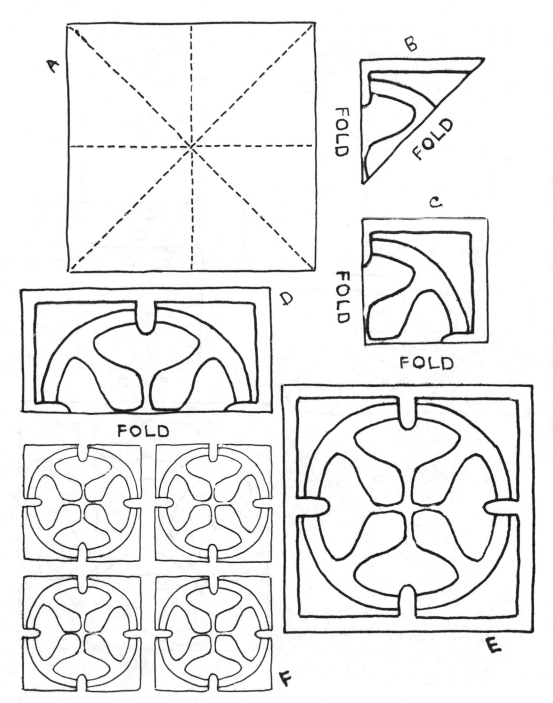

FIGURE 23. Based on same square as in Figure 22.

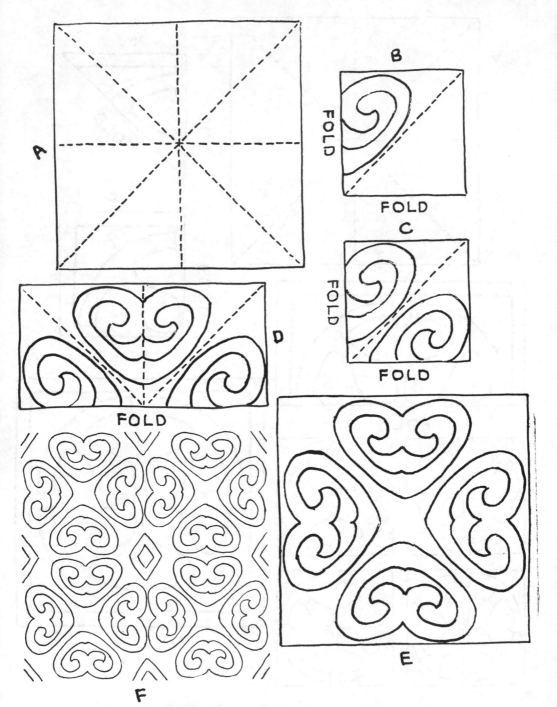

FIGURE 24. Geometric on square.

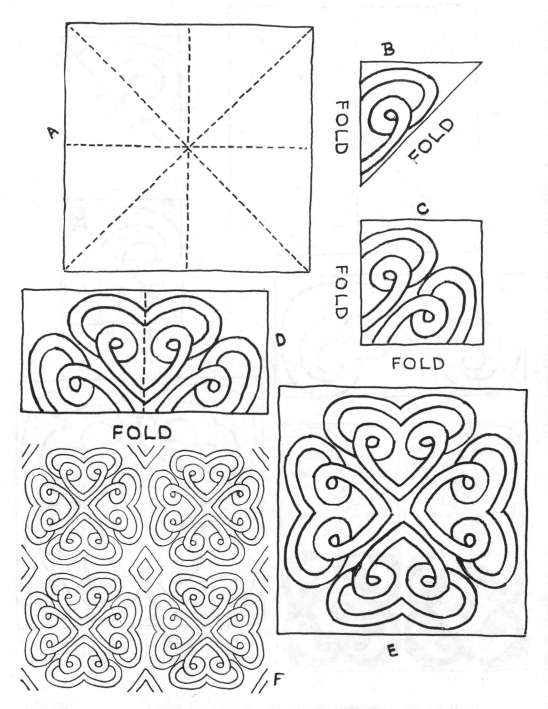

FIGURE 25. Geometric on square.

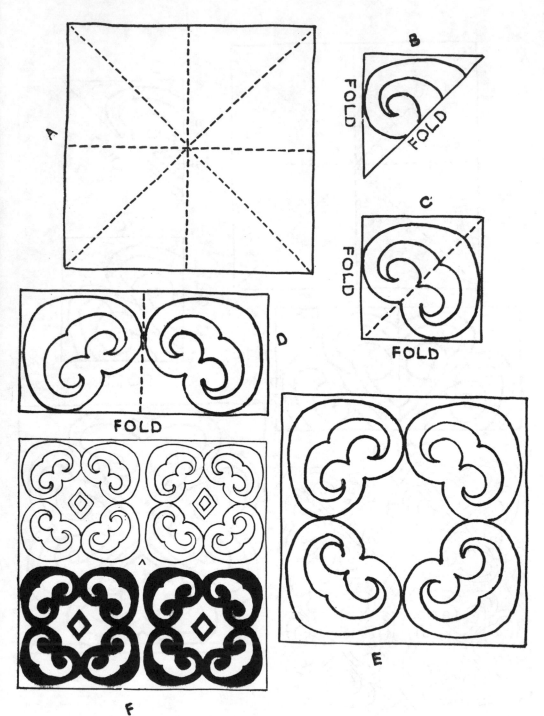

FIGURE 26. Geometric on square. F shows pattern both dark and light.

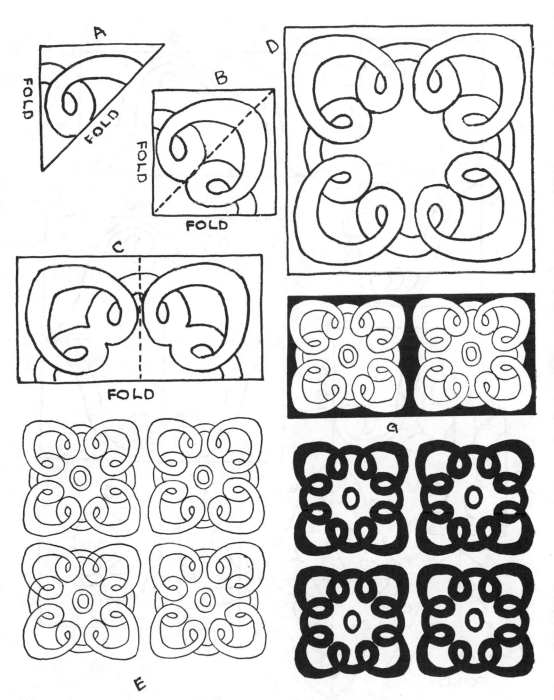

FIGURE 27. Geometric on square.

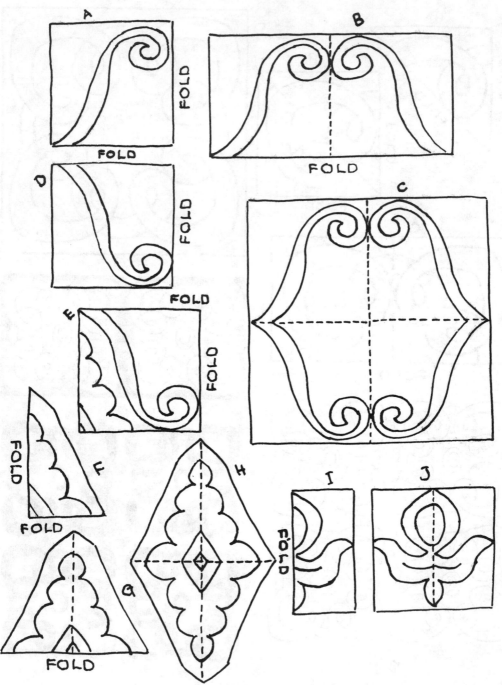

FIGURE 28. Finished, Fig. 30.

FIGURE 29A. Designs based on squares, on this and four next pages.

FIGURE 29B

[50]

FIGURE 29C

FIGURE 29D

FIGURE 29E

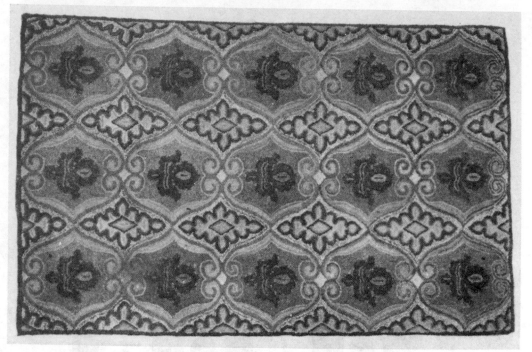

FIGURE 30. Worked out from the design shown in Figure 28.
HOOKED BY MRS. DAVID F. BATCHELDER.

PLANNING COLOR SCHEMES

Trace several units of your design on brown paper and try your color scheme with crayons. You can rub one color over another and get a variegated effect, making it darker and uneven in some places. Keep your color scheme up in front of you as you hook.

Do steps 7 and 8.

Figure 29 shows a number of designs based on a square.

Lesson 5
Fitting a Pattern to the Rug

MAKE a pattern for a rug, divide it into different spaces, and make designs to fit in these spaces.

Try one 27 inches wide and 70 inches long. A rug of this size will fit into many places and makes a nice hall runner.

1. From brown paper, cut a pattern this size or any size that you prefer. Put it on the floor to be sure it is the size you want. You may have to paste two or three pieces of paper together.

Next cut a pattern one fourth the size of the whole — 13½ inches wide and 35 inches long — or one fourth whatever size you want yours to be.

Divide the paper into three parts on the short side by creasing twice. Divide the paper into five parts on the long side by creasing four times.

The spaces will then be 4½ x 7 inches. Measure off some of these spaces and try different designs in them. See Figure 31. Do four units as shown in D, E, J, and K, making first one part dark and then the other. In this way you can see which part you like dark. Figures 32 and 33 show how two different halves of a completed rug would look with these two designs.

2. Divide your quarter into spaces 9 x 10 inches. You

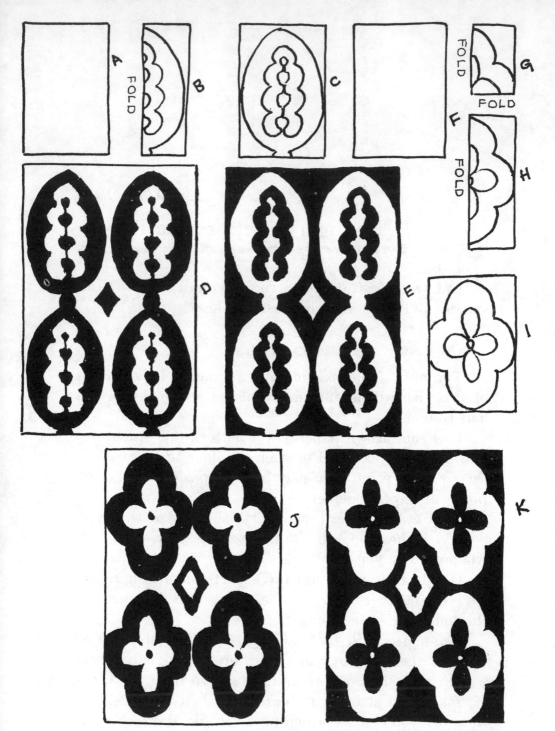

FIGURE 31. A—shows space. B—half of design in space. C—whole design. D—four of the units with one part dark. E—four of the units with opposite part dark, with diamond added where corner lines of spaces meet. F, G, H, I, J, K—second design, starting with one fourth at G.

[56]

FIGURE 33.　Half of a rug design, based on K, Figure 31.

FIGURE 32.　Half of a rug design, based on D, Figure 31.

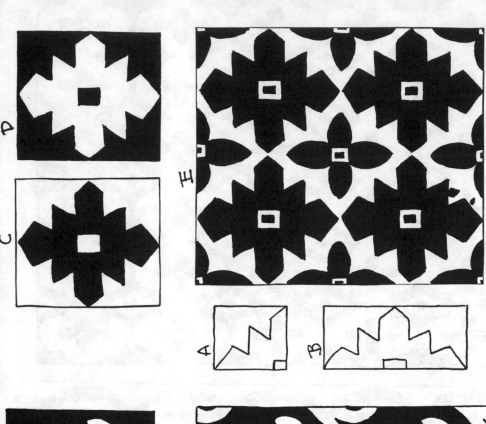

FIGURE 35. A—fourth of design unit. B—half of unit. C—whole unit in black. D—background in black. E—four units with design black and a four-sided, smaller unit put in between.

FIGURE 34. A—half of unit. B—whole unit in black. C—with background in black. D—four units with background in black, plus small unit added where lines of spaces meet.

FIGURE 36. Several designs to develop into a rug pattern.

FIGURE 38. Design suggestion.

FIGURE 37. A—half of design unit. B—whole unit with alternate parts dark. C—four units, and varied units to fill in dark spaces.

FIGURE 39. Design variation, in contrasting darks.

FIGURE 40. Possible pattern, in contrasting darks.

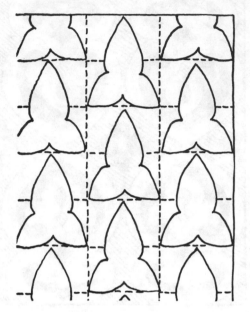

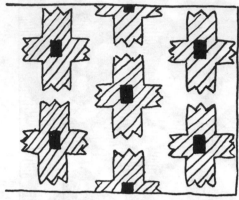

FIGURE 41. Note that in drop patterns, units are not on a line across the design.

will have 1½ spaces across and 3½ lengthwise. Figure 34 shows the development of a design in this space. Figure 35 shows another, and Figure 36 several designs. Use common ink or black crayon. You get the effect of how the dark and light will look very clearly this way. Put them down on the floor where you can see them. A design may look very well when done in line only, but when you get one part light and the other dark the defects stand out. Don't be too fussy about this, as you are just working for effect.

3. Next measure 9 inches; then 4½ inches across, in the same manner as when measuring the one before. Divide your lengthwise part into three parts by creasing twice. Your spaces will be 9 inches by a good 11⅝ inches. Figure 37 shows the development of a unit in this space. Half of the design is shown at A. Figures 38, 39, and 40 show different designs.

4. Divide quarter into spaces 9 x 14 inches. You will have 1½ spaces at the top and 2½ on the side.

5. Crease paper into three parts on the short side.

FIGURE 42. Attractive drop pattern adapted from leaf and vine design.

Divide into six parts on the long side by five folds.

This is to make a "drop" pattern. That is, half of every unit is below the next one to it. Figures 41, 42, and 43 explain this and show designs.

You see you can divide your rug up into any number of spaces to develop units in by taking a piece of paper one fourth the size of your rug and folding it to get the different sizes you want.

FIGURE 43. Drop pattern ideas in contrasting darks and lights.

Lesson 6
Using Flower Patterns

MAKE a rug divided into small squares with a floral motif in every other square and a circle with a small motif in the ones between. See Figure 44.

Make your first flowers in small squares or spaces. You have to think only about making your flower and do not have to consider how it is going to look beside other flowers.

PLANNING

Take 63 inches of yard-wide burlap and do steps 1, 2, and 3. From the center both ways measure 3⅜ inches, then 6¾ inches, till you have five spaces one way and nine the other. The outside measurements will be 33¾ x 60¾ inches.

DESIGNING

Cut some 6¾-inch squares of paper. (See examples at end of this lesson.) Take a piece of cretonne that you like, choose a flower and buds, and sketch them in one of your squares, using a piece of black marking crayon to draw with. See Figure 45A. Omit all detail, as it will disappear when you start hooking.

For the other square, with the circle design, take a saucer 4½ inches across and mark around it. See Figure 45B. In one circle, put a single flower. See Figure 45B. In the other put small flowers or berries and leaves. See

FIGURE 44. Square and circle design described in the text. For details, see Figures 45 and 46.

Figure 45C. Put "T" for top as shown in Figure 45.

Do steps 4 and 5. When you do 5, put crosses in every other square as shown in Figure 46B, and numbers in the others; then when you put your large design on, have the T at the top in space 1. When you come to 2, 3, and 4, have the T at the bottom. Then have it at the top for 5, 6, etc.

PLANNING COLOR SCHEME

You will need a lot of black or dark color for your background. I used three old skirts in mine and mixed them, as they were different.

Use bright colors for the flowers and buds, as they are small. You can use small scraps of color if you repeat two or three times. I used Egyptian red for one flower and had it very dark; and terra cotta for the other one, which I made lighter. For the other colors in that square, I used blue, orchid, and purple, with touches of rust. I used the same colors for the single flower and shades of blue for the berries in the other circle.

HOOKING

To do a good job in hooking flowers, you must cut your material in very narrow strips. Lay your cretonne sample on your rug where you can look at it and start on one of your large flowers. Try to copy the one in the cretonne. Put dark, light, and in-between colors where they fall in the sample.

Do not try to make your work look too well close to the job. When the finished rug is on the floor, you see it from a distance. Keep this fact in mind and from time to time stand off from your rug and look at it.

There is a dark and light part to every flower and there are dark accents. Get them in and do not bother too much about making the gradations even. With cretonne, one dark color is used for the dark accents all through the design. Try this.

Do not pull your first flower out. Let it alone. It may not look so well to you, but it will afterward. There is something that you put into your first flower that you do not always get into the ones you make afterward.

Do another flower, and make it darker or lighter. When two flowers are side by side, they should be of different degrees of intensity.

Do the buds and smaller flowers or berries. Make them darker toward the center and lighter on the outside.

When you make the leaves, copy some from the cretonne.

Do one square first, change colors in the next across if you want to, and have the last one on the end like the first one. Do the two with the circles in them and then

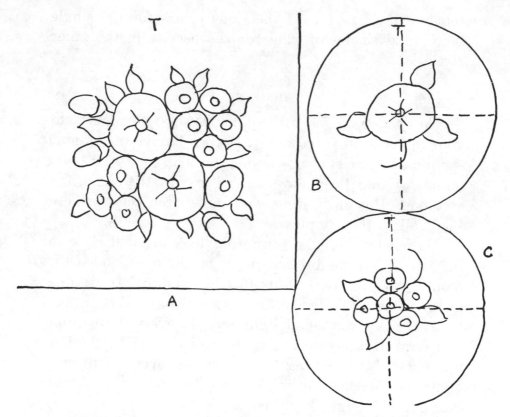

FIGURE 45. Units of the design shown in Figure 44.

go around the flowers and leaves with a row of white, which makes the design stand out.

Put your background in as you go along. Use plain or mixed colors.

I put in two rows of cream, a row of a color a little darker, then two rows of the first color, and so on. For the circles, I used the cream color.

I went around the circle with a row of black, then a row of light tan plaid and another row of black, and filled the rest in with black, hooking 'round and 'round. Where the lines met at the corners I made a small circle of black, then went around it with light brownish green.

Do steps 7 and 8.

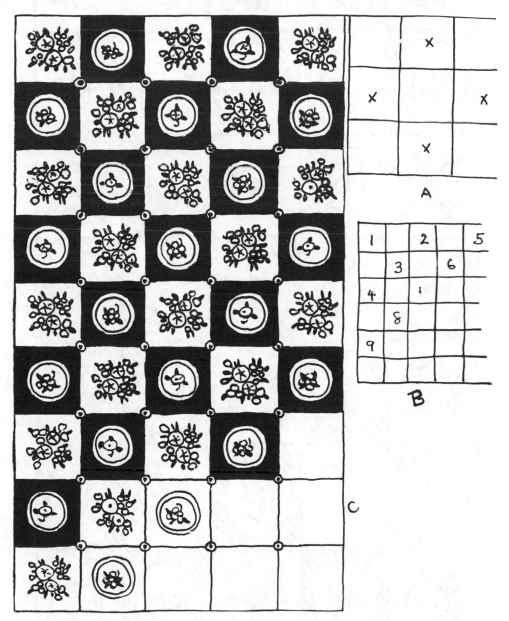

FIGURE 46. Making the pattern for the design shown in Figure 45.

FIGURE 47. Square and circle suggestion.

FIGURE 48. Square motif.

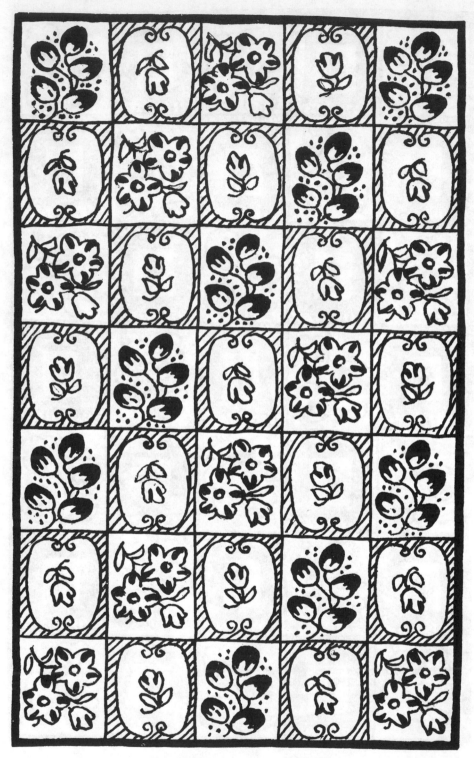

FIGURE 49. Square and circle.

[72]

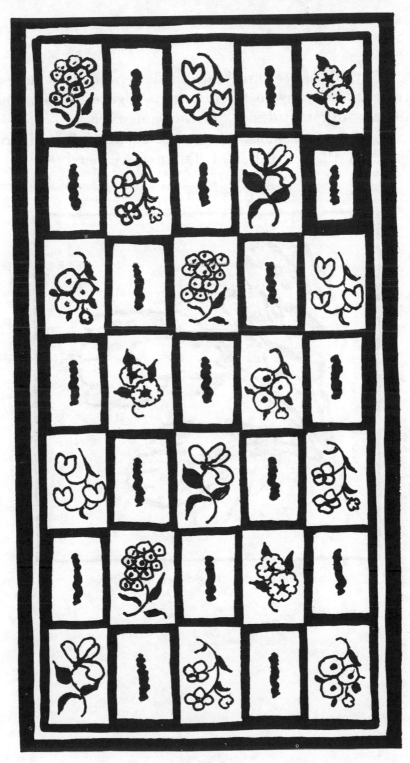

FIGURE 50. Oblongs as a variation.

[73]

You can use several kinds of flowers in the squares. It is an easy way to try a flower. Figures 47, 48, and 49 show different designs of the same type.

You can use oblongs instead of squares. See Figure 50. Note the five different designs used here.

Flower Idea for Square Pattern

Flower Ideas for Square Patterns

Flower Ideas for Square Patterns

Flower Ideas for Square Patterns

Flower Ideas for Square Patterns

Flower Ideas for Square Patterns

Flower Ideas for Square Patterns

[80]

Flower Idea for Square Pattern

Lesson 7
Geometric Based on a Circle

Mᴀᴋᴇ a geometric based on a circle, with flowers.
See Figure 51.

PLANNING

Take 31½ inches of 40-inch burlap and do steps 1, 2,
and 3. The selvedge edge in this rug will be at the sides
instead of at the top and bottom.

Starting at center and going toward selvedges both
ways, measure off 2 inches, then 4 inches.

From center going the other way, measure off 2¾
inches, then 5½ inches.

You will have nine spaces one way and five the other.
The outside measurements will be about 28 x 36 inches.

DESIGNING

Cut pieces of paper 4 x 5½ inches. Fold in middle
the short way and cut to make a scallop.

From pieces of cretonne or seed catalogues find
flowers that you can use in these spaces. Use large single
flowers; or two smaller ones or buds are nice to add.

Do steps 4, 5, and 6.

PLANNING COLOR SCHEME

Pastels would look well, and so would bright colors.
Do not have too much of any one color in any part.

I used rose, blue, orchid, yellow, violet, and a touch
of rust in mine.

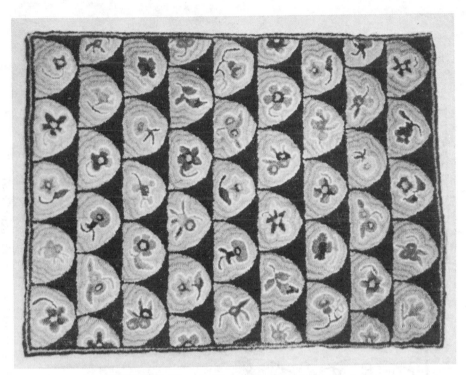

FIGURE 51. Arrangement of half ovals.

After I had the flowers and leaves done, I outlined them with a row of white, then put two rows of a light grayish tan, then a darker color, then two light and another row of the darker color where there was room, and then filled in all the rest, going 'round and 'round the flowers.

Cream would be nice for a background.

Fill in the rest with black or a dark color.

Figure 52 shows oblongs from which you can make various shapes based on an oval.

Figure 53 is a design worked up from the lines shown in oblong 2, Figure 52.

Figure 54 is a design worked up from the lines shown in oblong 3.

Figure 55 is a design worked up from the lines shown in oblong 4.

FIGURE 52. Basic units of the designs shown in Figures 53-57.

FIGURE 53. Worked up from 2, Figure 52.

[85]

FIGURE 54. Worked up from 3, Figure 52.

FIGURE 55. Worked up from 4, Figure 52.

FIGURE 56. Worked up from 5, Figure 52.

FIGURE 57. Worked up from 6, Figure 52.

FIGURE 58. Geometric based on a circle, with flowers.
See Figure 59. Described in the text. Author sold this to
McCall's and it was reproduced in the summer of 1943.—
PRINTED BY COURTESY OF THE MC CALL CORPORATION.

Figure 56 is a design worked up from the lines shown
in oblong 5.

Figure 57 is a design worked up from the lines shown
in oblong 6.

There are any number of ways that you can make
designs of this sort.

Figure 58 shows a design based on circles. Figure
59 shows an enlargement of one unit of a circle design.

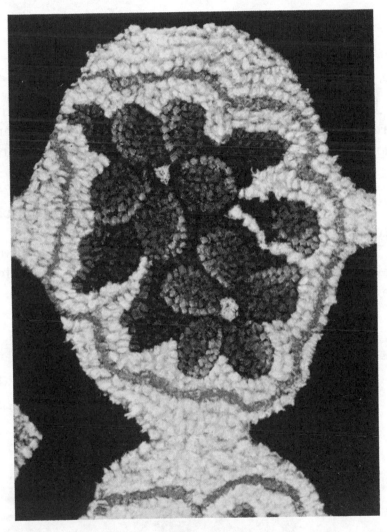

FIGURE 59. Enlargement showing detail of a geometric based on ovals.

Lesson 8
Chair and Stool Covers

Fᴏʀ round stool, make a pattern to fit your chair. Circles fit into some, but a square with the front corners rounded and the back not so wide goes better with others.

DESIGNING

Try a new flower and see how it is going to look before you place it against others in a rug.

Figure 60 shows one of my chair seats made to fit in a circle. Also see drawings, Figures 61-64. The circles are 14½ inches across.

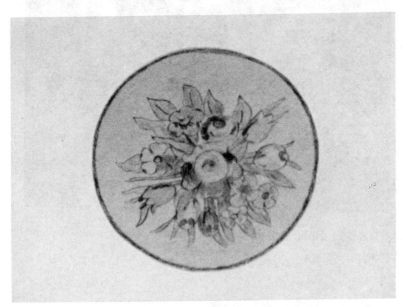

FIGURE 60. One of the author's chair-seat designs made to fit in a circle.

For designs to fit the regular chair-seat shape, see Figure 65.

SEAT AND BACK FOR BOSTON ROCKER

Make a design for a back and seat for a Boston rocker. See Figure 66.

PLANNING

You may want to make yours for some other type of chair, so make your pattern the size of the back and seat you have in mind.

Measure in all around on the back for your border, divide the center into six parts lengthwise, and then measure off the same distance the other way. Measure off the same distance border on the chair seat.

You can have the squares the same size as the back. Make a pattern for one square. Measure off your lines on your burlap and trace the design on.

You will see that there is a system to the color scheme.

A long strip for the floor would be stunning in this pattern.

Figure 67 — a cover for your piano bench and two stool covers.

Other suggestions are shown in the examples of designs that follow, Figure 68. The round one with the scalloped edge could be thrown over a round stool. Others are good for square and oblong stools and benches. Make these to fit any size stool.

Some people put four designs on a piece of burlap, put them in their frame, and do all four.

I use a small frame, just four strips of wood with listing on two sides, with clamps to fasten the corners together. I have seen a round embroidery hoop which would be nice to hook them in.

[93]

FIGURE 61. Round seat designs. Wreath with initial in center,
monogram, flowers in the center or going around the border or both.

FIGURE 62. Animal ideas for the round seat.

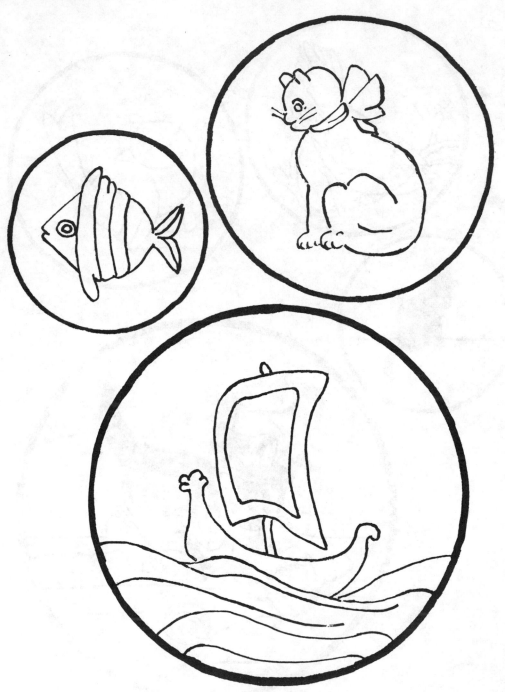

FIGURE 63. Animals and a boat.

FIGURE 64. Note silhouette effect at lower right.

FIGURE 65. Typical examples of designs for certain chair seats.

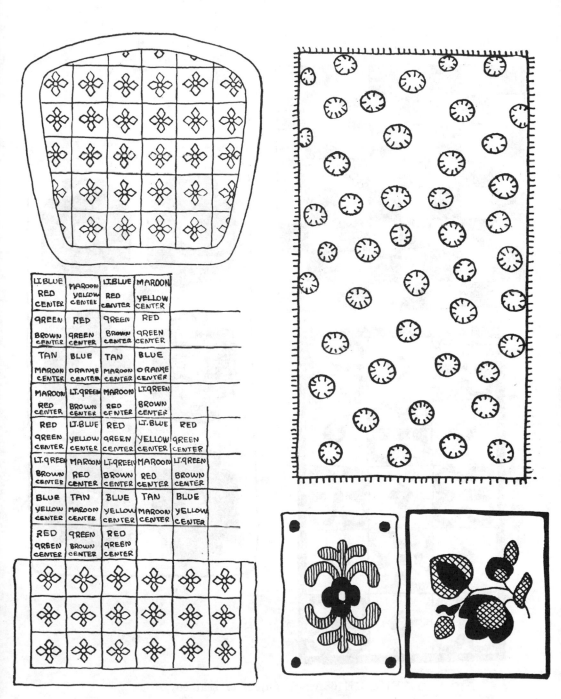

FIGURE 66. Seat and back design for Boston rocker.

FIGURE 67. Piano bench and other seat covers.

FIGURE 68A. Examples of seat covers.

FIGURE 68B. More seat covers.

Lesson 9
Planning Half-Round Rugs

Figure 69 shows a half-round rug the design of which I copied from a very thin, nearly worn-out rug which an antique dealer told me must be 150 years old.

The background was put in in straight lines from the front to the back instead of going 'round and 'round.

The scroll is red and there is a lot of it in the center.

The rug is 40 inches across at the back and 26 inches

FIGURE 69.   Half-round rug.—HOOKED BY MRS. DAVID F. BATCHELDER.

FIGURE 70B. More half-round suggestions.

FIGURE 70A. Suggestions for half-round designs.

A

B

C

FIGURE 71. Examples of Welcome rugs.

D

E

F

FIGURE 71 *(continued)*

the other way. I usually make my half-round rug designs 35¼ x 23 inches. Make your pattern the size of the place in which you want to put it.

Figure 70 shows seven designs you would like and which would be easy to make.

WELCOME RUGS

Welcome rugs are easy to make. First make your pattern of paper and try it where you are going to put your rug to be sure that it is all right. Then get your envelope of flowers out, draw two or three on small pieces of paper, and try them on your paper pattern. Pin them in place, sketch leaves around them, slip carbon paper under, and trace off.

Make two lines at the top for the word Welcome. Use any kind of letters that you want. Sketch them in roughly, and when you hook them do not try to make them too perfect. Make them look hand hooked.

Figure 71A-F shows six designs for Welcome rugs. I like the ones with the border of buds and leaves, very much. In this, you repeat the colors of the flowers you used inside.

Lesson 10

Planning a Hanging Motto

MAKE a motto to hang on the wall. Make a paper pattern and try it in the space where you want to hang your wall picture; the place where you want to hang it should govern the size.

DESIGNING

First decide on the motto that you want to use. You may have seen one that appealed to you in some old house.

Fold your paper both ways and get the center; then try folding your border. It's an easy way to find the size that you want. If you want a floral border, try folding about a sixth of the length of the paper from top to bottom. For a line or solid border you do not need to turn under so much. See Fig. 72.

Next make a line through the center from top to bottom. You must fit your motto into this space, and be sure to allow plenty of space for background all around.

Take a piece of paper the size you want the lettering to go in and try the words on this first. Get the middle lengthwise and arrange your words so that they are well placed on either side of this line. In "GOD BLESS OUR HOME," God goes on the top line so that the O is on the middle line; BLESS OUR makes nine letters — you count the space between words as one letter — so the S is on the middle line; HOME is four so you put the HO on one side and the ME on the other.

Make your letters fit in the same way on your pattern.

Divide the length of the space you are to fill, allowing an equal length for each row of lettering; space between each line of lettering, and have the margin a little wider at the bottom than the top and sides.

When the spacing suits you, draw lines across and sketch your letters in roughly with a black crayon.

You have to hook them, so make them simple and allow room for the thickness of the letters.

Now try designs for your border. You can have just lines or a solid color. If you do the latter, run a line of a light color around the inside like the beading on the inside of a picture frame.

Use leaves, simple buds, flowers, or anything else that may appeal to you.

When your design and border suit you, do steps 1, 2, 3, 4, 5, and 6.

HOOKING

Hook your letters first in black or any dark color. Stand off and look at it, and if your letters do not stand out enough make them heavier.

Put your background around them. Try to get a creamy or light tan effect.

Do your border next. If you use flowers and leaves, have the background darker than that used in the center. See Figure 72 for general plans.

You can also make just a circle or oval of flowers. Figure 73A shows one. The left half shows the plain design and the other is shaded. One half of this would make a nice Welcome rug design, or, instead of the traditional Welcome, why not say Enter? Or you could use this design for an oval rug and leave the center plain.

Figure 73B shows a basket of flowers set in a frame.

FIGURE 72. Examples of typical motto designs.

FIGURE 73. Wreath and "background" types of borders.

B

A

FIGURE 74

D

C

FIGURE 74 (*continued*)

F

E

FIGURE 74 (continued)

H

G

FIGURE 74 (*continued*)

J

I

FIGURE 74 (continued)

K

L

FIGURE 74 (continued)

You could make a floral bouquet. Figure 74A, B, and C shows flowers tied with a ribbon; Figure 74D, just two sprays with the stems crossed; Figure 74E, F, G, and H shows more flowers arranged the same way; Figure 74I, J, K, and L has the flowers arranged so that they could be used for wall hangings or for square rugs.

If you want to do something that's really fun, make a circle of all kinds of flowers and tie them with a bowknot. Make your pattern and draw a circle; then, starting from the bottom, put groups of good-sized flowers at the bottom and the sides, stick other flowers in, and add leaves and buds.

Black would look good on the outside and a light color on the inside. You could put your family name and the date you made it on the inside.

Lesson 11
Special Problems in Rugwork

To ENLARGE a design select a piece of paper large enough to take your design.

Draw a straight line at the bottom and up at the left.

Place the design you want to enlarge at the lower left-hand corner, and, with a straight-edge strip of wood or metal, draw a line from the corner of the design to the upper right of your paper, diagonally, as in A, Figure 75.

From the bottom line draw a line up to meet this diagonal line at the edge of the original design. Measure to be sure that it is straight. Where this line meets the diagonal line is the place for the top line. Measure this height, mark the left side, and draw the top line. See A, Figure 75. Enlargements are then based on the size and shape of the first oblong, by marking any point along the diagonal line. Several enlargements are shown.

Now you have the size that you want your design to be.

In actually enlarging the design, divide the original into squares. After you have divided the design into squares of equal size (see B), divide the larger space into the same number of squares (see C). Number the squares, beginning at a left-hand corner.

Just sketch what is in each square in the small one into the same square in the large one, to get your enlargement.

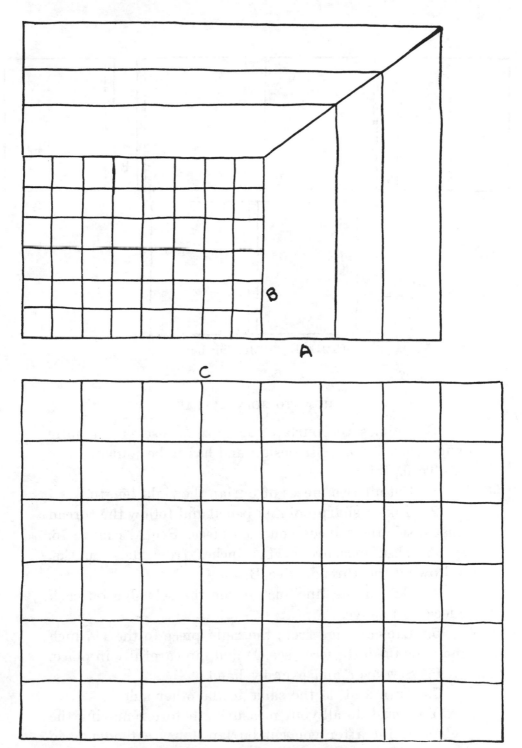

FIGURE 75. How to enlarge a design.

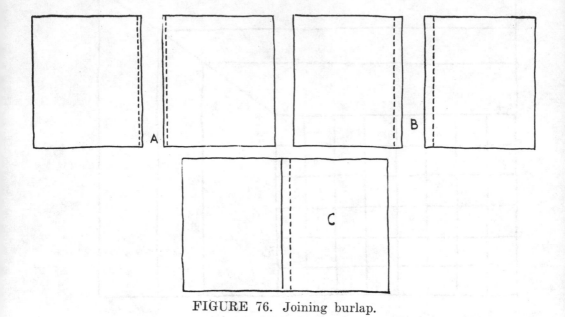

FIGURE 76. Joining burlap.

HOW TO JOIN BURLAP

Sometimes the burlap you have to use is not quite wide enough for your design and has to be joined.

To do this:

1. Cut off two pieces of burlap the right length.

2. Take a sharp-pointed pencil and follow the thread just inside the selvedge on each piece. See A, Figure 76.

3. Then measure in 1¼ inches from these marks, following the thread. See B.

4. Cut on the line just inside the selvedge on each piece, to remove.

5. Lap cut edge from the right piece to the 1¼-inch mark on the left piece (see C) and pin carefully in place.

6. Sew over and over by hand.

7. Turn and do the same to the other side.

You must do all your measuring before removing the selvedge, for after you cut burlap it has a tendency to fray and leave a ragged edge to measure from.

Don't fuss over your designs. Many times you get an idea and can't wait to get it on paper. Do it while you are in the mood, but know enough to stop at the right time! You'll do something and, instead of stopping when the creative mood is over, you go just a little bit farther and often spoil what you have done. It often happens that, in a first sketch done at white heat, there is something that you do not want to lose. It isn't the time that you put on a design, it's what you do in that time that counts.

Keep your designs simple. The simplest things are always best.

Be original. Make your own or adapt from others and have what you yourself like, regardless of what other people say.

Do not try to make your designs too perfect. It's handwork you are doing, so make it look that way.

The people who made oriental rugs deliberately made some little mistake because only Allah could do things perfectly! An authority on oriental rugs says that is one way they tell the genuine ones.

OUTSIDE THINGS TO CONSIDER IN MAKING A DESIGN

1. The place you plan to put your rug.

2. The colors used in the room you are going to put your rug in. Repeat in your rug some of the colors used in the room.

3. Do not try to cram too much into one design. You have to allow space to show off your design.

4. Avoid too much detail. If you start that way, you usually lose it in the hooking.

STYLE OF HOOKING

People are different; so is their hooking.

Have your own style and stick to it. Do not try to copy the other fellow exactly. When you have seen several of the paintings done by different artists, you can usually tell their work wherever you see it. You may not be a famous artist, but your work can be individual.

Some people cut their rags very, very fine. When their work is done you can kneel on the floor, look at it close, and it still looks like velvet. I am not in that class. I was taught in water-color work to get effect, to make your work look well at a distance.

It's up to you to choose your own style.

CARE OF HOOKED RUGS

We never beat our rugs. We put them on the grass, bottom side up, in the summertime and sweep them, then turn them over and sweep the tops. The rest of the time we sweep them topside up on the porch.

In winter, when you have a dry, powdery snow, before the sun melts it, put your rugs on a porch or other smooth surface, bottom side up, and throw some of the snow on. Then sweep it off, turn your rug over, and do the same thing to the top several times. The snow will be discolored and you will be amazed to see how much better your rugs will look.

This is the way we clean our rugs. It's old fashioned but it works.

DYEING

Get good dyes that are easy to use and will not stain your hands.

You can take the color out of material that you want to dye by putting a very little soda in water. Put your material in and bring it to a boil; then rinse well. Do not let your material stay in too long or it will rot.

It's easier to make a flower if you have the different gradations of color. Try a little at first in a small kettle. Put a piece in and let it boil a few minutes; then add another, and another, and so on, and, when you think the strength of the dye is all used up, put in one more piece for your very lightest tints.

When dry, arrange them on a table or back of a chair and see if you have good gradations of color. If you need more, try again.

You can tie knots in your material as they do in tie-and-dye work.

Do not try to make your dyed work even. It's much more effective if it comes out streaked and uneven.

WORKING SUGGESTIONS

1. Artists work in a north light. Do the same.

2. A corner in your kitchen makes an ideal studio. A plain wood table or a board spread across two chairs is all you need to make your designs on and put them on burlap. When you get ready to hook, use the same place, and, if you can have your rug all ready to work on whenever you have a few spare minutes, you can get a lot more done.

3. Work on your rug the first thing in the morning when you are fresh. You can accomplish twice as much then and everything seems to go right.

4. Go into churches and look at the stained-glass windows at different times of the day and see the changing effects. Our rugs should be like that. Some will get lots of sunlight and some will stay more in the shadows.

5. Do not be too disturbed over the criticism you receive from well-meaning friends and start pulling out each thing that someone does not like. Did you read the fable of the man, the boy, and the donkey when you went to school? You can never please everyone, so try to please

yourself. It is your creation, you are making it, and you are going to use it when it is finished.

6. *Never use anything but wool in your rugs.*

7. Remember to keep repeating your theme color. Keep in mind what I said in Lesson 1. You must have a theme color — just as you hear a recurrent theme in a symphony, so you have a color that you keep repeating at intervals throughout your rug.

8. Try to see your rug as a whole design, not as separate flowers or units.

Lesson 12
Planning Good Borders

Borders are really the frames for your rugs.

It's a simple matter to plan a border to go within two straight lines, but you have to turn a corner and that is the problem.

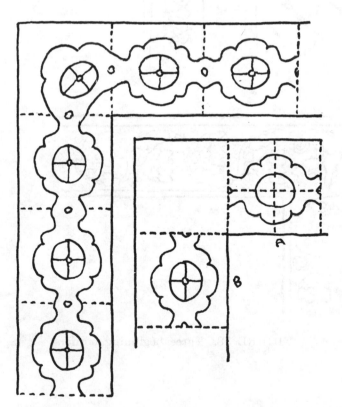

FIGURE 77. Steps in making a border design.

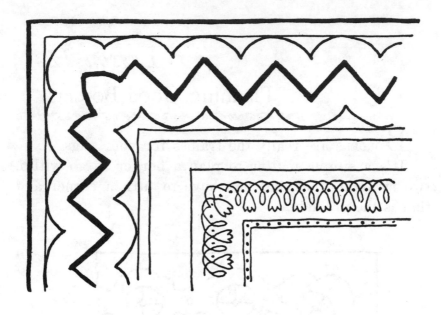

FIGURE 78. Three beginning borders.

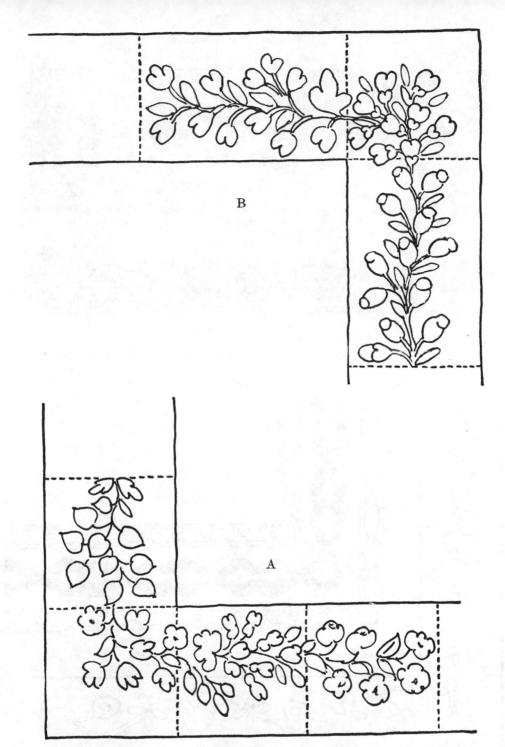

FIGURE 79. A. Three different designs that can be used in succession with the same corner. Can be cut in any unit and the effect will be all right. B. Very easy. Just alternate the motif. Buds and berries give chance for lots of color.

FIGURE 80. A rich design created and hooked a long time ago by the author. Note interest of the border on the inside and around the outside.

FIGURE 81. Knotted string and tendril design. Leaves may be added to the latter.

FIGURE 82. Two borders you will like to do. With the flower border, use the same flowers as in the center. If you want a black background, remember to keep the tips of the leaves light and to have dark enough in the center to balance the black in the background. If you use a light background, make it darker than the one in the center and have a dark line on either side. The fruit border may be treated the same way.

FIGURE 83. A border that turns the corner by continuing on around. Would be very effective with a dark or black background.

Borders and centers must differ — borders with small figures, centers with one or several large figures.

To make a border: 1. Measure off one fourth of the size of your rug. 2. Decide on the width of the border. Mark off into spaces. See Figure 77. 3. Cut paper size one space. 4. Crease lengthwise, allowing more space from center to outer edge than from center to inside edge.

FIGURE 84. Has been made with design in one space light tan, outlined with faded red, almost a pink. In the next space, the outline pink is used for the inside, with brownish red on the outside. The background, dark brown (very old looking). Centers of all the flowers and bands at either side, light. Dots in border, reddish brown. Would also be stunning in shades of old gold with a black background.

5. Make several of these. When one suits you, transfer to A and B, Figure 77. 6. Then draw in corner so that the design flows gracefully from one unit to the other. 7. Trace on the unit in the other spaces. Remember to allow more space on the outer side of your design than on the inside. Do nearly every border this way.

A border can simply be lines but with the spaces between the lines of different widths, the widest space on the outside, the narrowest next, and the in-between first. An easy way to remember it is to say 2, 3, 1.

Do not use a solid color. Mix your shades from light to dark, with the dark toward the outside. Separate the lines by a dark color used in the center, or by black.

FIGURE 85. Using the border shown in Figure 86.—HOOKED BY
MRS. DAVID F. BATCHELDER.

Figures 78 and 79 show five easy beginning patterns
for borders. Figure 80 shows the contrast in shades of
a good design, and the effect of a border design with a
plain center. See Figures 81, 82, 83, and 84 for ideas on
different types of borders.

Figure 85 illustrates the popular rug with the border
shown in Figure 86.

See Figure 87 for a good border with inset of a detail
from it.

When you make a special size rug and your border is
too long for the sides or end, make your corners the same
and do the changing at the ends and sides.

FIGURE 86.   The author's most popular border. For finished effect, see Figure 85. First, mark off the border all around, and then put in the construction lines. Designed for 36-inch burlap.

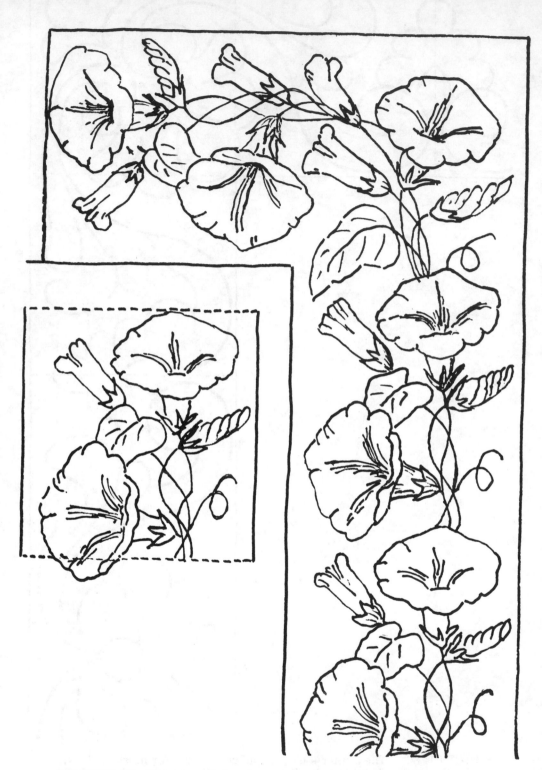

FIGURE 87. Morning glory border. One you would like to make.
Fill any bare spaces with a tendril. In a flower border, the stems of
the flowers make a line which carries the eye around the entire rug.

Special Problems
Floral and Other Designs

Dᴇsɪɢɴ your floral rugs the way it is easiest for you.

I do not draw my flowers on my pattern; I sketch them in on small pieces of brown paper, then put carbon paper under and trace off a number of each kind.

I can put these on my pattern and try them first one way and then another. When I like the arrangement, I pin them in place and sketch leaves around them, then slip carbon paper under each flower and trace it off onto the brown paper. I use this pattern to transfer the design to the burlap.

FIGURE 88. First of examples hooked with author's popular "dahlia" pattern. (Roses in the center.)

FIGURE 89. Same design, except for border, as Figure 88.—HOOKED BY MRS. FORREST CHASE.

Sometimes I color several of the flowers and the leaves in. After I have the design all traced on, I take these separate flowers and put them in an envelope and mark on it the name of the rug.

For special orders, I often take different envelopes of flowers, arrange them right on the burlap, and trace them onto it.

Figure 88 — I got all the flowers for this rug from one piece of cretonne. I call this my "dahlia" rug.

Figure 89 — The same design with dark background.

Figure 91 — The same flowers with a simple, narrow border. I have a half-round rug using them.

FIGURE 90. Simplified pattern.—HOOKED BY MRS. FORREST CHASE.

FIGURE 91. The same flowers, with narrow border.

FIGURE 92. Dahlia pattern, combined with the popular border shown in Figure 86. Here the center pattern has been extended as told in the text.—HOOKED BY MRS. HERBERT PAGE.

FIGURE 93. Same center, with several variations. — HOOKED BY MRS. DAVID F. BATCHELDER.

FIGURE 94. Rose pattern, a little large for the rug.

Figure 92 — A neighbor wanted a rug to go into a certain place and she liked the border in Figure 86, so I put that one on. I cut a paper pattern the size of the center and tried my "dahlia" pattern in it and liked it, only it was not long enough. So I traced the center and ends of the "dahlia" design, pinned some flowers and buds on the in-between part, and then traced them on.

Checkered material was used for the border and center background. That gives it that variegated effect and holds the border and center together.

Figure 93 — My mother wanted to use my same center but preferred to try different flowers in the rest of the rug.

Figure 94 — These are different roses. I added more buds as I hooked and got the center larger than I had planned. This rug could stand a wider border.

FIGURE 95. Rose pattern with an effective black background.—
HOOKED BY MRS. HERBERT PAGE.

Figure 95 — The same roses, only the design is smaller than the one I made. A neighbor made this, using a black background.

Figure 96 — A child called this my "balloon" rug and the name stuck. I used nearly all new flowers for this. The border has just a curved line with circles and the colors used in the center are repeated in these circles.

Instead of the circles, leaves, buds, or flowers could be used.

Figure 97 — A rug my mother hooked which we use as a wall hanging. The border is very fine and delicate. I drew it in freehand.

FIGURE 96. The "balloon" rug. All new flowers.

FIGURE 97. A fine floral design, with an exquisite, freehand border.
—HOOKED BY MRS. DAVID F. BATCHELDER.

FIGURE 98. Many kinds of flowers could be used here.

FIGURE 99. Here the border becomes the main part of the design.

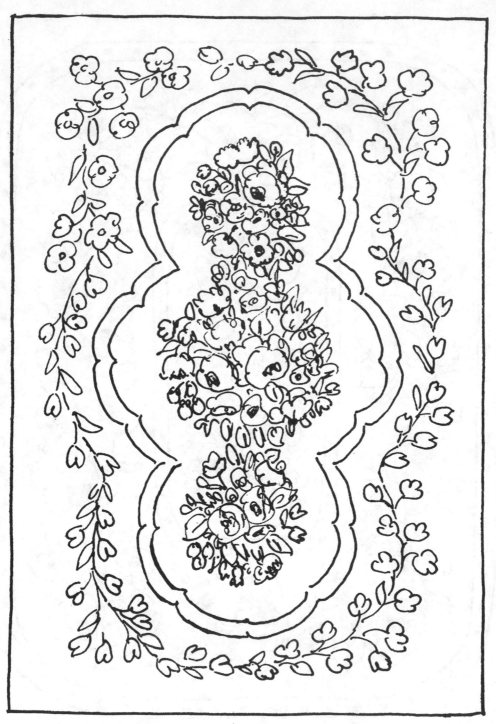

FIGURE 100. A floral worked out in three parts.

[144]

FIGURE 101. Oval and curved-line combination.

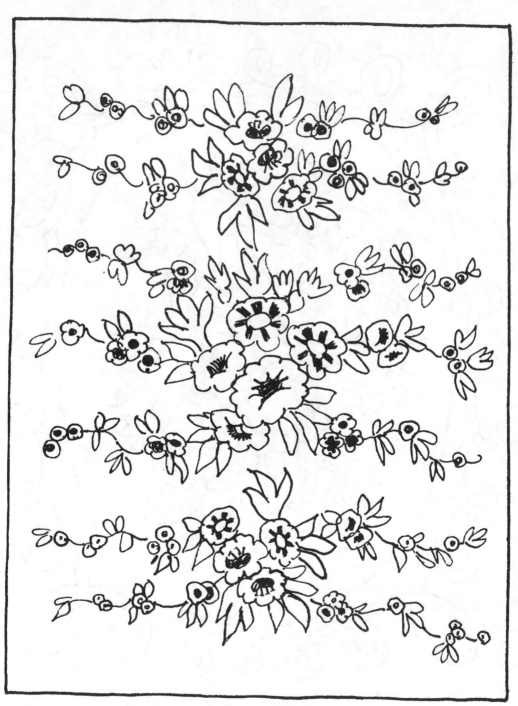

FIGURE 102. A different type of design.

FIGURE 103. ''Corsage''-type decoration.

FIGURE 105. Possible floral grouping with great appeal.

FIGURE 104. To suggest how a square rug with big flower center would look.

[148]

FIGURE 106. Flowers and scrolls, in a rich pattern.

Here are some sketches for floral rugs.

Figure 98 has a floral center, a wide floral border, and flowers in the corners. You could use all kinds of flowers in this. A black background would make the flowers stand out.

Figure 99 shows a poppy rug — lots of poppies going around the border and in the center, too, with plenty of buds. Buds are very easy to make and very effective. If you have a bare space, it's a good idea to add a bud.

There are two other kinds of flowers and the two bands around have oval spots which give you a chance to add the colors used in the center and in the extra-wide "border."

In Figure 100, the center is divided into three parts, surrounded by a scalloped band with flowers outside.

FIGURE 107. Another highly decorative flower-and-scroll design.— HOOKED BY MRS. DAVID F. BATCHELDER.

The sketch Figure 101 has an oval in the center with curved lines around it.

Figure 102 shows groups of flowers, one in the center and one at either end. Stems go out from these with flowers, then stems and more flowers. It's different but it would be fun to do.

Figure 103 shows flowers in the center surrounded by leaves, with ribbons going in opposite directions. A third ribbon could be added. A border of bands of the colors used in the center could be added, also.

Figure 104 suggests the effect of a square rug with big flowers, and Figure 105 a simple arrangement that would be very effective. Omit corner designs if you wish.

Figure 106 — An oval with scrolls. Scrolls are easy to do. Sketch one link and trace a number of others from it. Arrange them around your center.

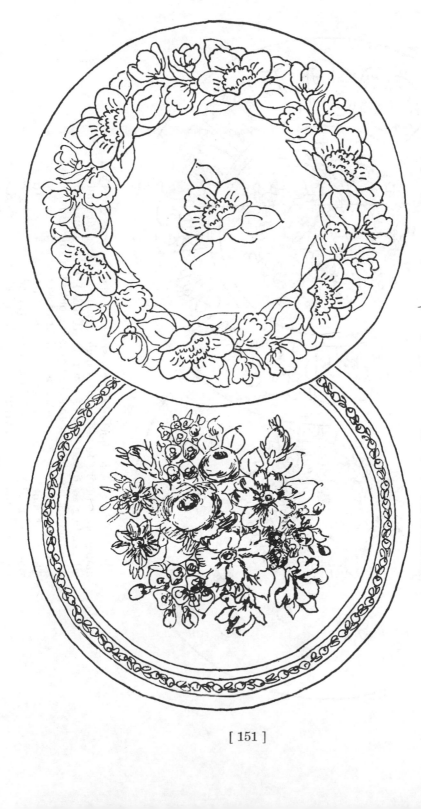

FIGURE 108 A platelike pattern based on flowers, leaves, and bands.

FIGURE 109.. Purely floral. Make one sixth of the finished wreath and transfer to fill the rest.

FIGURE 110. A bouquet of flowers, surrounded with leaves gives you ample opportunity to use color. Single flowers scattered around are all heading in different directions. FIGURE 111. A round center with flowers, then a band and oblongs going out from this with sprays of different flowers. You could use a light background in the center. The band could be shades of some color used in the center. (Green would be good.) The oblongs could be outlined with a dark color from the center; the background in them kept light but a little darker than that used in the center. The band outside could be like the band inside.

[152]

FIGURE 112. Flowers of any kind, and loops, in a pretty though formal effect.

You need something in the corners when your scrolls form an oval.

Figure 107 — Flowers in center, scrolls around.

There is a charm about the curved lines in round and oval rugs. You can get lots of ideas for these from dishes. I once saw a design for an oval rug for a dining room taken from the dishes the lady used.

Figures 108-116 will give you a number of suggestions for floral designs. I am especially fond of the geometrics, Figures 117 and 118, so am including them to round out your selections. There are many places where rugs of this sort look well.

FIGURE 113. Dahlia and scroll design, with tulips and other flowers, in oval shape.

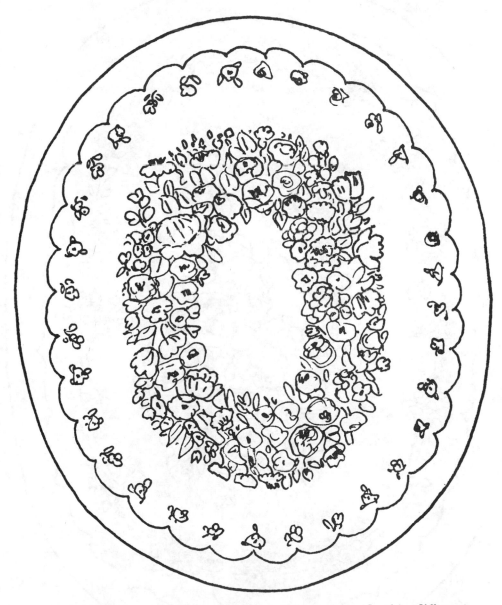

FIGURE 114. Scallops around the edge, and, inside this, different kinds of flowers. A wider band could go around the center of the wreath, and more flowers added.

FIGURE 115. A long oval in the center. Bouquets of flowers going around the edge, with leaves connecting them.

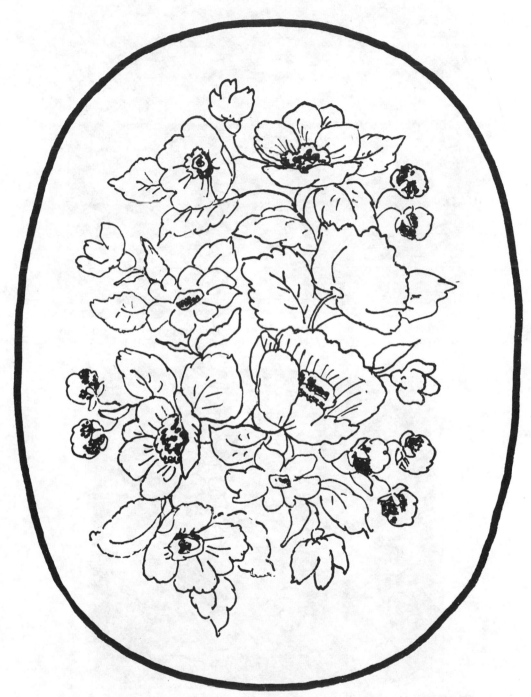

FIGURE 116. An unusual, spacious arrangement for a poppy center.

FIGURE 117. A favorite geometric of the author's.—STITCHED BY
MRS. DAVID F. BATCHELDER. (Could be hooked just as well.)

FIGURE 118. Another favorite geometric, very simple in plan.—
HOOKED BY MRS. DAVID F. BATCHELDER.

Index to Illustrations

INDEX